To: _____

From: _____

THE HELEN STEINER RICE FOUNDATION

God knows no strangers, He loves us all,
The poor, the rich, the great, the small.
He is a Friend who is always there
To share our troubles and lessen our care.
No one is a stranger in God's sight,
For God is love and in His light
May we, too, try in our small way
To make new friends from day to day.

Whatever the celebration, whatever the day, whatever the event, whatever the occasion, Helen Steiner Rice possessed the ability to express the appropriate feeling for that particular moment in time.

A happening became happier, a sentiment more sentimental, a memory more memorable because of her deep sensitivity to put into understandable language the emotion being experienced. Her positive attitude, her concern for others, and her love of God are identifiable threads woven into her life, her work . . . and even her death.

Prior to her passing, she established the HELEN STEINER RICE FOUNDATION, a nonprofit corporation whose purpose is to award grants to worthy charitable programs that aid the elderly, the needy, and the poor. In her lifetime, these were the individuals about whom Mrs. Rice was greatly concerned.

Royalties from the sale of this book will add to the financial capabilities of the HELEN STEINER RICE FOUNDATION, thus making possible additional grants to various qualified, worthwhile, and charitable programs. Because of her foresight, her caring, and her deep convictions, Helen Steiner Rice continues to touch a countless number of lives. Thank you for your assistance in helping to keep Helen's dream alive.

Virginia J. Ruehlmann, Administrator
The Helen Steiner Rice Foundation
Suite 2100, Atrium Two
221 E. Fourth Street
Cincinnati, Ohio 45201

Helen Steiner Rice

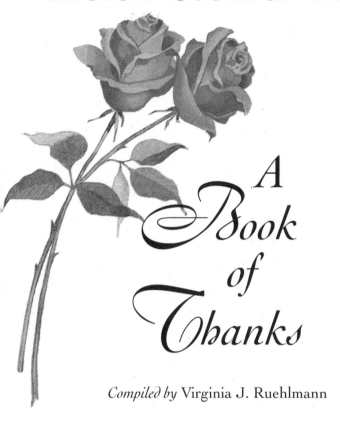

A
Book
of
Thanks

Compiled by Virginia J. Ruehlmann

Fleming H. Revell
A Division of Baker Book House Co
Grand Rapids, Michigan 49516

© 1993 by Virginia J. Ruehlmann and
The Helen Steiner Rice Foundation

Published by Fleming H. Revell
a division of Baker Book House Company
P.O. Box 6287, Grand Rapids, MI 49516-6287

Fourth printing, April 1995

Printed in the United States of America

Library of Congress Cataloging-in-Publication Data

Rice, Helen Steiner.
    A book of thanks / Helen Steiner Rice : compiled by Virginia J. Ruehlmann.
      p.   cm.
   ISBN 0-8007-1695-7
    1. Christian poetry, American. I. Ruehlmann, Virginia J. II. Title.
PS3568.I28B66 1933
811'.54--dc20   93-3967

Illustrations by Jack Brouwer

Scripture references marked RSV are taken from the Revised Standard Version of the Bible, copyright 1946, 1952, 1971, and 1973 by the Division of Christian Education of the National Council of the Churches of Christ in the United States of America.

Scripture references marked TEV are from the *Good News Bible*—Old Testament: Copyright American Bible Society 1976; New Testament: Copyright American Bible Society 1966, 1971, 1976.

Scripture quotations marked NASB are from the New American Standard Bible, the Lockman Foundation 1960, 1962, 1963, 1968, 1971, 1972, 1973, 1975, 1977.

Scripture quotations marked KJV are from the King James Version of the Bible.

Dedicated
with grateful appreciation to
Andrea R. Cornett
and Dorothy C. Lingg
for their untiring and conscientious service to
The Helen Steiner Rice Foundation
and to each individual
who possesses and expresses
an attitude of gratitude

Contents

Introduction

I remember years ago singing to our young children and teaching them the song "There Are Two Little Magic Words."

Perhaps you recall it:

> There are two little magic words
> That will open every door with ease.
> One little word is *thanks*
> And the other little word is *please.*
> You'll be so surprised
> What these two little words can do.
> They worked like a charm for me
> And they'll work like a charm for you.
>
> AUTHOR UNKNOWN

I loved that song as well as the lesson that it taught. The world would be nicer if, as adults, we continued the practice of saying: Thank you, Grazie, Danke schön, Gracias, Merci, Tack, Dank, Asante, Kansha suru, Spasi'bo.

It makes no difference which language is written or spoken; *thank you* is always appreciated and understood. Such an expression is good to offer and wonderful to receive! It boosts the morale, creates a smile, and often prompts a hug, a kiss, or an embrace.

Helen Steiner Rice used her ability to convey gratitude in an easy-to-comprehend, rhythmic flow of words. She simply, and yet eloquently, expressed appreciation to God and to acquaintances, friends, and readers for a variety of blessings and kindnesses. May you enjoy the many ways in which she put her heartfelt thanks into written form, and may all of us add *thank you* many times to our daily vocabularies.

Appreciatively,
Virginia J. Ruehlmann

It is good to give thanks to the Lord, to sing praises to thy name, O Most High . . . For thou, O Lord, hast made me glad by thy work; at the works of thy hands I sing for joy.

Psalm 92:1, 4 RSV

Thank You, God

A *Prayer of Thanks*

Thank You, God, for the beauty
    around me everywhere,
The gentle rain and glistening dew,
    the sunshine and the air,
The joyous gift of feeling
    the soul's soft, whispering voice
That speaks to me from deep within
    and makes my heart rejoice.

Everywhere across the land, we see God's face and touch His hand.
This thought and all the thoughts in this book are by Helen Steiner Rice.

Showers of Blessings

Each day there are showers of blessings
   sent from the Father above,
For God is a great, lavish giver,
   and there is no end to His love.
His grace is more than sufficient,
   His mercy is boundless and deep,
His infinite blessings are countless—
   and all this we're given to keep
If we but seek God and find Him
   and ask for a bounteous measure
Of this wholly immeasurable offering
   from God's inexhaustible treasure.
For no matter how big man's dreams are,
   God's blessings are infinitely more,
For always God's giving is greater
   than what man is asking for.

How will we use these days and the time God has placed in our hands? Will we waste the minutes and squander the hours, leaving no prints behind in time's sands?

$\mathcal{N}$ever Despair—
God's Always There!

In sickness or health,
in suffering or pain,
In storm-laden skies,
in sunshine and rain
God always is there
to lighten your way
And lead you through darkness
to a much brighter day.

In this wavering world of unbelief, we are filled with doubt and questioning fear. Oh, give us faith in things unseen, so we may feel Thy presence near.

The *Mystery* and Miracle of His Creative Hand

In the beauty of a snowflake
   falling softly on the land
Is the mystery and the miracle
   of God's great, creative hand.
What better answers are there
   to prove His holy being
Than the wonders all around us
   that are ours just for the seeing?

Father, make us kind and wise, so that Your blessings we may recognize.

Where Can We Find Him?

It's true we have never looked on God's face,
But His likeness shines forth from every place,
For the hand of God is everywhere
Along life's busy thoroughfare,
And His presence can be felt and seen
Right in the midst of our daily routine.
The things we touch and see and feel
Are what make God so very real.

The silent stars in timeless skies,
The wonderment in children's eyes,
The gossamer wings of a hummingbird,
The joy that comes from a kindly word,
The autumn haze, the breath of spring,
The chirping song that crickets sing,
A rosebud in a slender vase,
A smile upon a friendly face.

In everything both great and small
We see the hand of God in all,
And every day somewhere, someplace,
We see the likeness of His face.
For who can watch a new day's birth
Or touch the warm life-giving earth
Or feel the softness of the breeze
Or look at skies through lacy trees
And say they've never seen His face
Or looked upon His throne of grace?

Thank You, God, for Little Things

Thank You, God, for little things
    that often come our way,
The things we take for granted
    but don't mention when we pray—
The unexpected courtesy,
    the thoughtful, kindly deed,
A hand reached out to help us
    in the time of sudden need.
Oh, make us more aware, dear God,
    of little daily graces
That come to us with sweet surprise
    from never-dreamed-of places.

Life is twice as nice when thoughtful things folks do and say, make every day a special day.

My Garden of Prayer

My garden beautifies my yard
  and adds fragrance to the air,
But it is also my cathedral
  and my quiet place of prayer.
So little do we realize
  that the glory and the power
Of Him who made the universe
  lie hidden in a flower!

You can't touch a rose all fragrant with dew without part of the fragrance remaining with you.

It's a Comfort to Know

O, God, what a comfort
to know that You care,
And to know when I seek You
You will always be there.

*It's amazing and incredible, but it's as true as it can be, God loves
and understands us all and that means you and me!*

He Made the Sun

God made the sun,
  He made the sky,
He made the trees
  and the birds that fly.
God made the flowers,
  He made the light,
He made the stars
  that shine at night.
God made the rain,
  He made the dew,
And He made
  special friends like you!

Our Father made the heavens, the mountains and the hills, the rivers and the oceans, and the singing whippoorwills.

Thank You, God

Thank You, God, for everything
   I've experienced here on earth,
Thank You for protecting me
   from the moment of my birth,
Oh, God, no words are great enough
   to thank You for just living,
And that is why every day
   is a day for real thanksgiving.

*Everything that's wonderful is but a rich reward, given to us
lovingly by a gracious, generous Lord.*

The Golden Key

To be in God's keeping
   is surely a blessing,
For though life is sometimes
   dark and distressing,
No day is too dark
   and no burden too great
That God in His love
   cannot penetrate.
And to know and believe
   without question or doubt
That no matter what happens
   God is there to help out,
Is to hold in your hand
   the golden key
To peace and to joy
   and serenity!

Never give up and never stop, continue on to the mountaintop.

A Friend Is a Gift from God

Among the great and glorious gifts
  our heavenly Father sends
Is the gift of understanding
  that we find in loving friends,
For in this world of trouble
  that is filled with anxious care,
Everybody needs a friend
  in whom they're free to share
The little secret heartaches
  that lay heavy on the mind,
Not just a mere acquaintance,
  but someone who's just our kind.
For somehow in the generous heart
  of loving, faithful friends,
The good God in His charity
  and wisdom always sends
A sense of understanding
  and the power of perception
And mixes these fine qualities
  with kindness and affection.

So when we need some sympathy
  or a friendly hand to touch
Or one who listens tenderly
  and speaks words that mean so much,
We seek a true and trusted friend
  in the knowledge that we'll find
A heart that's sympathetic
  and an understanding mind,
And often just without a word
  there seems to be a union
Of thoughts and kindred feelings,
  for God gives true friends communion.

Precious Little Memories

Precious little memories
   of little things well done,
Make the very darkest day
   a bright and happy one.
Tender little memories
   of some word or deed,
Give us strength and courage
   when we are in need.
Blessed little memories
   help us bear the cross
And soften all the bitterness
   of failure and of loss.
Priceless little memories
   are treasures without price,
And through the gateway of the heart
   they lead to paradise.

Memories are priceless possessions that time can never destroy, for it is in happy remembrance that the heart finds its greatest joy.

It's a Wonderful World

A warm, ready smile
 or a kind, thoughtful deed,
Or a hand outstretched
 in an hour of need
Can change our whole outlook
 and make the world bright
Where a minute before
 just nothing seemed right.
It's a wonderful world,
 and it always will be
If we keep our eyes open
 and focused to see
The wonderful things
 we are capable of
When we open our hearts
 to God and His love.

Hearts are made a little lighter and darkest days a little brighter by thank-you notes that play a part in lighting candles in the heart.

What More Can You Ask?

God's love endureth forever —
　　what a wonderful thing to know
When the tides of life run against you
　　and your spirit is downcast and low.
God's kindness is ever around you,
　　always ready to freely impart
Strength to your faltering spirit,
　　cheer to your lonely heart.
God's presence is ever beside you,
　　as near as the reach of your hand,
You have but to tell Him your troubles,
　　there is nothing He won't understand.
So wait with a heart that is patient
　　for the goodness of God to prevail,
For never do prayers go unanswered,
　　and His mercy and love never fail.

Only the knowledge that we're understood makes everyday living feel wonderfully good.

Take Time to Be Kind

Kindness is a virtue
   given by the Lord.
It pays dividends in happiness,
   and joy is its reward.
For if you practice kindness
   in all you say and do,

The Lord will wrap His kindness
   all around your heart and you.
And wrapped within His kindness
   you are sheltered and secure,
And under His direction
   your way is safe and sure.

So Many Reasons
to Love the Lord

Thank You, God, for little things
    that come unexpectedly
To brighten up a dreary day
    that dawned so dismally.
Thank You, God, for sending
    a happy thought this way
To blot out my depression
    on a disappointing day.
Thank You, God, for brushing
    the dark clouds from my mind
And leaving only sunshine
    and joy of heart behind.
Oh, God, the list is endless
    of things to thank You for,
But I take them for granted
    and unconsciously ignore
That everything I think or do,
    each movement that I make,
Each measured rhythmic heartbeat,
    each breath of life I take

Is something You have given me
for which there is no way
For me in all my smallness
to in any way repay.

God's Everlasting Gift

We all have many things
    to be deeply thankful for,
But God's everlasting promise
    of life forevermore
Is a reason for thanksgiving
    every hour of the day
As we walk toward eternal life
    along the King's highway.

We all make mistakes—it's human to err—but no one need ever give up in despair, for God gives us all a brand-new beginning, a chance to start over and repent of our sinning.

Thank You, God, for Everything

Thank You, God, for everything,
  the big things and the small,
For every good gift comes from God,
  the Giver of them all,
And all too often we accept
  without any thanks or praise
The gifts God sends as blessings
  each day in many ways.
Thank You for the miracles
  we are much too blind to see,
And give us new awareness
  of our many gifts from Thee,
And help us to remember
  that the key to life and living
Is to make each prayer a prayer of thanks
  and every day Thanksgiving.

Remembering You is pleasant to do, for there is always joy in thanking You.

In every thing give thanks.

1 Thessalonians 5:18 KJV

A
Thankful Heart

There Is a Reason for Everything

Our Father knows what's best for us,
    so why should we complain?
We always want the sunshine,
    but He knows there must be rain.
We love the sound of laughter
    and the merriment of cheer,
But our hearts would lose their tenderness
    if we never shed a tear.
Our Father tests us often
    with suffering and with sorrow.
He tests us not to punish us
    but to help us with tomorrow.
For growing trees are strengthened
    when they withstand the storm,
And the sharp cut of a chisel
    gives the marble grace and form.
God never hurts us needlessly,
    and He never wastes our pain,
For every loss He sends to us
    is followed by rich gain.
And when we count the blessings
    that God has so freely sent,

We will find no cause for murmuring
   and no time to lament,
For our Father loves His children,
   and to Him all things are plain,
So He never sends us pleasure
   when the soul's deep need is pain.
So whenever we are troubled
   and when everything goes wrong,
It is just God working in us
   to make our spirits strong.

Be Glad!

Be glad that you've had such a full, happy life,
Be glad for your joy as well as your strife,
Be glad that you've walked in sunshine and rain,
Be glad that you've felt both pleasure and pain,
Be glad that you've tasted the bitter and sweet,
Be glad that your life has been full and complete,
Be glad that you've walked with courage each day,
Be glad that you've had strength for each step of
   the way,
Be glad for the comfort you've found in prayer,
But be gladdest of all for God's tender care.

Blest are they who walk in love. They also walk with God above.

There Are Blessings in Everything

Blessings come in many guises
    that God alone in love devises,
And sickness, which we dread so much,
    can bring a very healing touch.
For often on the wings of pain
    the peace we sought before in vain
Will come to us with sweet surprise
    for God is merciful and wise.
For through long hours of tribulation
    God gives us time for meditation,
And no sickness can be counted loss
    that teaches us to bear our cross:

*There can be no crown of stars without a cross to bear, and there is
no salvation without faith and love and prayer.*

Look on the Sunny Side

There are always two sides,
   the good and the bad,
The dark and the light,
   the sad and the glad,
But in looking back over
   the good and the bad,
We're aware of the number
   of good things we've had.
And in counting our blessings,
   we find when we're through
We've no reason at all
   to complain or be blue.
So thank God for the good things
   He has already done,
And be grateful to Him
   for the battles you've won,
And know that the same God
   who helped you before
Is ready and willing
   to help you once more.
Then with faith in your heart,
   reach out for God's hand

And accept what He sends,
   though you can't understand,
For our Father in heaven
   always knows what is best,
And if you trust His wisdom,
   your life will be blessed.
For always remember
   that, whatever betide you,
You are never alone,
   for God is beside you.

$\mathcal{D}$on't Be Discouraged

It's easy to grow downhearted
   when nothing goes your way.
It's easy to be discouraged
   when you have a troublesome day.
But trouble is only a challenge
   to spur you on to achieve
The best that God has to offer
   if you have the faith to believe!

Just like a sunbeam makes a cloudy day brighter, a friend makes a heavy heart lighter.

The Gift of Friendship

Friendship is a priceless gift
   that cannot be bought or sold,
But its value is far greater
   than a mountain made of gold,
For gold is cold and lifeless,
   it can neither see nor hear,
And in the time of trouble,
   it is powerless to cheer.
It has no ears to listen,
   no heart to understand,
It cannot bring you comfort
   or reach out a helping hand.
So when you ask God for a gift,
   be thankful if He sends
Not diamonds, pearls, or riches
   but the love of real, true friends.

And he who gives of himself will find true joy of heart and peace of mind.

Expectation! Anticipation! Realization!

God gives us a power we so seldom employ
    for we're so unaware it is filled with such joy,
For the gift that God gives us is anticipation,
    which we can fulfill with sincere expectation.
And there's power in belief when we think we will find
    joy for the heart and sweet peace for the mind,
For believing the day will bring a surprise
    is not only pleasant but surprisingly wise.
For we open the door to let joy walk through
    when we learn to expect the best and most too,
And believing we'll find a happy surprise
    makes reality out of a fancied surmise!

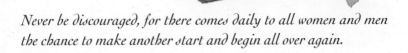

*Never be discouraged, for there comes daily to all women and men
the chance to make another start and begin all over again.*

A Recipe for Happiness

Happiness is something
   we create in our mind,
It's not something you search for
   and so seldom find,
It's just waking up
   and beginning the day
By counting our blessings
   and kneeling to pray.
It's giving up thoughts
   that breed discontent
And accepting what comes
   as a gift heaven-sent.
It's giving up wishing
   for things we have not
And making the best of
   whatever we've got.
For it's by completing
   what God gives us to do
That we find real contentment
   and happiness, too.

*I meet God in the morning and go with Him through the day,
then in the stillness of the night, before sleep comes, I pray.*

Not by Chance or Happenstance

Into our lives come many things
   to break the dull routine,
The things we had not planned on
   that happen unforeseen,
The unexpected little joys
   that are scattered on our way,
Success we did not count on
   or a rare, fulfilling day,
A catchy, lilting melody
   that makes us want to dance,
A nameless exaltation
   of enchantment and romance,
An unsought word of kindness,
   a compliment or two
That set the eyes to gleaming
   like crystal drops of dew,
The unplanned sudden meeting
   that comes with sweet surprise
And lights the heart with happiness
   like a rainbow in the skies.

Now some folks call it fickle fate
   and some folks call it chance,
While others just accept it
   as a pleasant happenstance.
But no matter what you call it,
   it didn't come without design,
For all our lives are fashioned
   by the hand that is divine.
And every happy happening
   and every lucky break
Are little gifts from God above
   that are ours to freely take.

Grant Us Wisdom

God, grant us grace to use
   all the hours of our days
Not for our own selfish interests
   and our own willful ways,
But teach us to take time for praying
   and for listening to You,
So each day is spent wisely
   doing what You want us to.

*Do you pause in meditation upon life's thoroughfare, and offer up
thanksgiving, or say a word of prayer?*

Why Am I Complaining?

My cross is not too heavy,
　　my road is not too rough,
Because God walks beside me
　　and to know this is enough.
And though I get so lonely,
　　I know I'm not alone,
For the Lord God is my Father
　　and He loves me as His own.
So though I'm tired and weary
　　and I wish my race were run,
God will only terminate it
　　when my work on earth is done.
So let me stop complaining
　　about my load of care,
For God will always lighten it
　　when it gets too much to bear.
And if He does not ease my load
　　He will give me strength to bear it,
For God in love and mercy
　　is always near to share it.

*It takes a lot of living to fully realize that all God's greatest bless-
ings come to us in a disguise.*

Beyond Our Asking

More than hearts can imagine
    or minds comprehend,
God's bountiful gifts
    are ours without end.
We ask for a cupful
    when the vast sea is ours,
We pick a small rosebud
    from a garden of flowers,
We reach for a sunbeam,
    but the sun still abides,
We draw one short breath,
    but there's air on all sides.
Whatever we ask for
    falls short of God's giving,
For His greatness exceeds
    every facet of living,
And always God's ready
    and eager and willing

To pour out His mercy
  completely fulfilling
All of man's needs
  for peace, joy, and rest
For God gives His children
  whatever is best.
Just give Him a chance
  to open His treasures
And He'll fill your life
  with unfathomable pleasures,
Pleasures that never
  grow worn-out and faded
And leave us depleted,
  disillusioned, and jaded,
For God has a storehouse
  just filled to the brim
With all that man needs
  if we'll only ask Him.

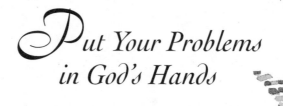

Put Your Problems in God's Hands

Although it sometimes seems to us
    our prayers have not been heard,
God always knows our every need
    without a single word,
And He will not forsake us
    even though the way is steep,
For always He is near to us,
    a tender watch to keep.

May you know the comfort of God's all-fulfilling grace and love.

A Simple Prayer of Thanksgiving

I come not to ask, to plead, or implore You,
  I come to tell You how much I adore You,
For to kneel in Your presence makes me feel blest
  For I know that You know all my needs best,
And it fills me with joy just to linger with You
    As my soul You replenish and my heart You
    renew,
For prayer is much more than asking for things,
    it's the peace and contentment that quietness
    brings.
So thank You again for Your mercy and love
  and for making me heir to Your kingdom above!

God's mighty hand can be felt every minute, for there is nothing on earth that God isn't in it.

Quit Supposin'

Don't start your day by supposin'
   that trouble is just ahead,
It's better to stop supposin'
   and start with a prayer instead.
And make it a prayer of thanksgiving
   for the wonderful things God has wrought,

Like the beautiful sunrise and sunset,
 God's gifts that are free and not bought.
For what is the use of supposin'
 the dire things that could happen to you
And worry about some misfortune
 that seldom if ever comes true?
But instead of just idle supposin'
 step forward to meet each new day
Secure in the knowledge God's near you
 to lead you each step of the way.
For supposin' the worst things will happen
 only helps to make them come true,
And you darken the bright happy moments
 that the dear Lord has given to you.
So if you desire to be happy
 and get rid of the misery of dread
Just give up supposin' the worst things
 and look for the best things instead.

Adversity Can Distress Us or Bless Us

If we observe the miracles
    that happen every day,
We cannot help but be convinced
    that in His wondrous way
God makes what seemed unbearable
    and painful and distressing
Easily acceptable
    when we view it as a blessing.

Offer thanks when you walk in sunshine and rain or experience both pleasure and pain.

The Richest Gifts

The richest gifts
  are God's to give,
May you possess them
  as long as you live,
May you walk with Him
  and dwell in His love
As He sends you good gifts
  from heaven above.

When it comes to showing appreciation, I can't find words to express the many things I thank You for, but You understand, I guess.

A *Thankful Heart*

Take nothing for granted,
   for whenever you do
The joy of enjoying
   is lessened for you
For we rob our own lives
   much more than we know
When we fail to respond
   or in any way show
Our thanks for the blessings
   that daily are ours,
The warmth of the sun,
   the fragrance of flowers,
The beauty of twilight,
   the freshness of dawn,
The coolness of dew
   on a green velvet lawn,

The kind little deeds
  so thoughtfully done,
The favors of friends
  and the love that someone
Unselfishly gives us
  in myriad ways,
Expecting no payment
  and no words of praise.
Oh, great is our loss
  when we no longer find
A thankful response
  to things of this kind,
For the joy of enjoying
  and the fullness of living
Are found in the heart that is
  filled with thanksgiving.

Then on that day David first assigned
Asaph and his relatives to give thanks to the
LORD: "Oh give thanks to the LORD, call
upon His name; make known His deeds
among the peoples." . . . Then all the people
said, "Amen," and praised the LORD.

1 Chronicles 16:7, 8, 36 NASB

Holidays Are Thank-You Days

A *New Year's Meditation*

What better time
  and what better season,
What greater occasion
  or more wonderful reason,
To kneel down in prayer
  and lift our hands high
To the God of creation,
  who made earth and sky,
Who sent us His Son
  to live here among men,
And the message He brought
  is as true now as then.
So at this glad season,
  when there's joy everywhere,
Let us meet our Redeemer
  at the altar of prayer,
Asking Him humbly
  to bless all of our days
And grant us forgiveness
  for our erring ways.
And though we're unworthy,
  dear Father above,

Accept us today
   and let us dwell in Thy love,
So we may grow stronger
   upheld by Thy grace,
And with Thy assistance
   be ready to face
All the temptations
   that fill every day.
And hold on to our hands
   when we stumble and stray.
And thank You, dear God,
   for the year that now ends
And for the great blessing
   of loved ones and friends.

One Nation under God

Thanksgiving is more
    than a day in November
That students of history
    are taught to remember,
For while we still offer
    the traditional prayer,
We pray out of habit
    without being aware
That the Pilgrims thanked God
    just for being alive,
For the strength that He gave them
    to endure and survive.
We tend to forget
    that our forefathers came
To establish a country
    under God's name.

Oh, teach us, dear God,
   we are all Pilgrims still,
Subject alone to
   Your guidance and will,
And show us the way
   to purposeful living
So we may have reason
   for daily thanksgiving.

To Our Founding Fathers

Faith of our fathers, renew us again
And make us a nation of God-fearing men
Seeking Thy guidance, Thy love, and Thy will,
For we are but Pilgrims in search of Thee still.
And, when gathered together on Thanksgiving Day
May we lift up our hearts and our hands as we pray
To thank You for blessings we so little merit,
And grant us Thy love and teach us to share it.

Often through the passing days, we feel deep down inside unspoken thoughts of thankfulness and fond, admiring pride.

There Is Cause for Rejoicing

May the holy remembrance
   of that first Christmas Day,
Be our reassurance
   that Christ is not far away,
For on Christmas He came
   to walk here on earth,
So let us find joy
   in the news of His birth,
And let us find comfort
   and strength for each day
In knowing that Christ walked
   this same earthly way.
He knows all our needs,
   and hears every prayer,
And He keeps all His children
   safe in His care.
So once more at Christmas,
   let the whole world rejoice
In the knowledge He answers
   every prayer that we voice.

May the love of God surround you, may His peace be all around you.

God So Loved the World

Our Father up in heaven,
   long, long years ago,
Looked down in His great mercy
   upon the earth below
And saw that folks were lonely
   and lost in deep despair
And so He said, "I'll send My Son
   to walk among them there,
So they can hear Him speaking
   and feel His nearness, too,
And see the many miracles
   that faith alone can do.
For if man really sees Him
   and can touch His healing hand
I know it will be easier
   to believe and understand."

And so the Holy Christ Child
    came down to live on earth
And that is why we celebrate
    His holy, wondrous birth,
And that is why at Christmas
    the world becomes aware
That heaven may seem far away
    but God is everywhere.

*O*ur Thanks for the Gift
of Go*d's* Love

All over the world at this season,
    expectant hands reach to receive
Gifts that are lavishly fashioned,
    the finest that man can conceive.
For, purchased and given at Christmas
    are luxuries we long to possess,
Given as favors and tokens
    to try in some way to express
That strange, indefinable feeling
    which is part of this glad time of year
When streets are crowded with shoppers
    and the air resounds with good cheer.

But back of each tinsel-tied package
    exchanged at this gift-giving season,
Unrecognized often by many,
    lies a deeper, more meaningful reason,
For, born in a manger at Christmas
    as a gift from the Father above,
An Infant whose name was called Jesus
    brought mankind the gift of God's Love.
And the gifts that we give have no purpose
    unless God is part of the giving,
And unless we make Christmas a pattern
    to be followed in everyday living.

Thanks for Remembering

Ever since Christmas I've been thinking of you
　with deep appreciation and fond affection, too,
Thinking I was lucky beyond what words could say
　to be remembered by you in such a lovely way,
Thinking as I often do, that I am truly blest
　in knowing lovely folks like you who stand out
　　from the rest,
Thinking I'm not worthy of honors such as this
　and wishing I could tell you with a grateful hug
　　and kiss,
Just how much you pleased me and just how much
　it meant
　to get your priceless Christmas gift, I'm sure was
　　heaven-sent,
And through the year I'll often think with loving
　thankfulness
　how much your nice gift added to my Christmas
　　happiness.

*Nothing on earth can make life more worthwhile than "thanks"
from a friend with the warmth of a smile.*

No Words to Thank You

Each year when Christmas comes,
   you do so much for me,
I find myself just overwhelmed
   and thankful as can be.
I want to say so very much,
   but haven't words to thank you,
In fact, I want to kiss you,
   and yet I ought to spank you.
But if my heart could tell you
   all the gratefulness I feel,
You'd know my thanks to all of you
   was deep and true and real.
But more than any gift from you,
   I prize your friendly thought,
And you'll never know the pleasure
   that your friendliness has brought!

*I can never pay you for your cherished gift and thought, but I can
thank you with my heart for the inner joy it brought.*

This Is What Christmas Is All About

Christmas to me is a gift from above,
    a gift of salvation born of God's love,
For far beyond what my mind comprehends,
    my eternal future completely depends
On that first Christmas night centuries ago
    when God sent His Son to the earth below.
For if the Christ Child had not been born
    there would be no rejoicing on Easter morn,
For only because Christ was born and died
    and hung on a cross to be crucified
Can worldly sinners like you and me
    be fit to live in eternity.
So Christmas is more than getting and giving,
    it's the why and the wherefore of infinite living,
It's the positive proof for doubting God never,
    for in His kingdom life is forever.
And that is the reason that on Christmas Day
    I can only kneel down and prayerfully say,
"Thank You, God, for sending Your Son
    so when my work on earth is done,
I can look at last on Your holy face,
    knowing You saved me alone by Your grace!"

thank
you
so
much

Belated Thanks

What can I tell you??? What can I say???
I'm filled with thanks . . . and also dismay . . .
Thanks that I haven't expressed to date
And great dismay because I'm so late.

But always, it seems, through the holidays
I get helplessly lost in a muddled maze,
And all of the things I mean to do
Are left undone and unfinished, too.

Of course, it's true the holidays tire us
And this year, I've had the virus . . .
So instead of being just naturally slow
This virulent virus knocked me low!

All I can say is thank you so much
For adding once more your cheerful touch
And just as always your dainty selection
Was the very acme of pretty perfection!

Thank-you notes are links of love sent to friends we're fondest of.

Every good gift and every perfect present comes from heaven; it comes down from God, the Creator of the heavenly lights.

James 1:17 TEV

Thanks for What You Have Given

Life's Gift of Love

If people like me
   didn't know people like you,
Life would lose its meaning
   and its richness, too,
For the friends that we make
   are life's gift of love,
And I think friends are sent
   right from heaven above,
And thinking of you
   somehow makes me feel
That God is love
   and He's very real.

Among the great and glorious gifts our heavenly Father sends, is the gift of understanding that we find in loving friends.

Faith

I prize your friendship,
   I treasure your love,
I believe in you
   and in God above,
And knowing this
   should help you win
And finish each task
   that you begin
And give you courage
   to see you through,
For I am with you
   in all that you do,
So have the faith
   that I have in you,
And things will turn out
   as you want them to.

All the good wishes a heart can make are sent today for friendship's sake.

Things to Be Thankful For

The good, green earth beneath our feet,
   the air we breathe, the food we eat,
Some work to do, a goal to win,
   a hidden longing deep within
That spurs us on to bigger things
   and helps us meet what each day brings—
All these things and many more
   are things we should be thankful for.

*You cannot bring happiness into the lives of others without
spreading a little of it inside your own heart.*

Life's Richest Treasures

It's not the things that cost a lot
    that are life's richest treasure,
It's priceless little courtesies
    that money cannot measure.
It's some gracious little gesture,
    some kindly, little favor
That fills the heart with gratitude
    and adds that friendly flavor.
And in spite of life's vexations
    and irritations too,
It's heart-warming and refreshing
    to meet nice folks like you,
For people of the kind like you
    help make life worth living
And give us reason in this world
    for a bit of real thanksgiving.

You give me things that cannot be purchased with silver and gold,
for thoughtfulness and kindness are never bought or sold.

Friendly Faces

It takes more than high-class merchandise
   and beautiful decor,
To make a place of business
   something more than just a store,
For it is not glittering garnishments
   that sparkle in the cases,
It's the welcome, warmth, and courtesy
   that shine from friendly faces.

Thank you for the nice things you do the whole year through.
May they come back multiplied many times to you.

In His Footsteps

When someone does a kindness,
    it always seems to me
That's the way God up in heaven
    would like us all to be.
For when we bring some pleasure
    to another human heart,
We have followed in His footsteps
    and we've had a little part
In serving Him who loves us,
    for I'm very sure it's true
That in serving those around us,
    we serve and please Him, too.

When deeply distraught, forget your own despair and reach out to help others who need your care.

God Speaks

When I looked at those flowers,
  I was looking at God,
For they bloomed in His sun
  and grew in His sod,
And each lovely flower
  was a voice from above
That whispered a message
  of kindness and love.
For I felt in my heart,
  and I know you do, too,
That God speaks to us all
  through the kind things we do,
And when I looked at those flowers,
  I couldn't help but feel
That they brought heaven nearer
  and made God so real.

In the tiny petal of a tiny flower, that grew from a tiny pod, is the miracle and the mystery of all creation and God!

A *Gift* of Love

When I opened the beautifully wrapped gift,
My first impulse was a smothered, "Oh, this is too
  much!"
But somehow, since talking with you and observ-
  ing you,
I have come to recognize that your great generosity
Is born of great gratitude
And your great gift of love and understanding
Is born of a thankful heart!

Happiness is just a state of mind within the reach of everyone who takes the time to be kind.

This Is Too Much!

The elegant sweater of a fabulous brand
  is much too expensive and much, much too
    grand!
It's lovely to look at and so soft to the touch,
  but I firmly maintain this is much too much!

*Rare gifts always fill me with mixed emotions . . . they make my
heart sing and they sober my soul at the same time. I am always
deeply touched and very humbled and overwhelmed with awe.*

A Rose Is a Rose

The flowers came,
  and they're lovely indeed,
But if you had sent only
  a twig and a weed
They'd have looked
  just beautiful to me,
For beyond what
  my aging eyes can see,
I would have felt the love
  that inspired the sending,
And that is
  beauty unending!

Like roses in a garden, kindness fills the air, with a certain bit of sweetness as it touches everywhere.

$\mathcal{I}$ Was Never So Delighted

My dear friend, I was never so delighted,
Never so completely pleased and never more
   excited!
You couldn't have sent me anything that meant as
   much to me
As petals from "the cross of Christ" made from the
   dogwood tree.
My dear friend, you're an angel in disguise,
For only someone very blessed could make such a
   lovely surprise.
I've hunted everywhere in a vain attempt to find
Some sprays of heavenly dogwood that were just the
   perfect kind.
And now, I'm very anxious to place them in a vase
And see how beautiful they look, by my Madonna's
   face.
And every time I look at them, I'm sure that I will
   see
The face of someone wonderful who's been so nice
   to me,
And the face belongs to someone I admire very
   much,
Who has the ways of an angel and also a heavenly
   touch,

And, of course, you are the angel that I am speak-
ing of,
For everything you ever do is done with tender love.
You put so much of yourself into your lovely flowers,
You share your talent and your strength, your
efforts and your hours,
And always with no thought of praise or any thought
of pay,
But always with but one idea—to brighten some-
one's day.
And may it please you to know these dogwood
sprays
Are more than a thing of beauty, they're really an
anthem of praise.
And always a quiet reminder of that sacred and
beautiful story
That only by carrying the cross of Christ can we
reach the kingdom's glory!

The Musings of
a Thankful Heart

People everywhere in life
   from every walk and station
From every town and city
   and every state and nation,
Have given me so many things
   intangible and dear,
I couldn't begin to count them all
   or even make them clear.
I only know I owe so much
   to people everywhere
And when I put my thoughts in verse
   it's just my way to share
The musings of a thankful heart,
   a heart much like your own,
For nothing that I think or write
   is mine and mine alone.

So if you found some beauty
in any word or line
It's just your soul's reflection
in proximity with mine.

Thank You to the Artist

The portrait is very lovely
   the work of an artist, it's true,
But the touch is the touch of a sensitive heart
   and hands skilled and sensitive, too.
Of course, being human, I'm flattered
   you gave me an eye-catching face,
But one thing I treasure the deepest,
   that nothing can ever erase,
Is to think that you wanted to do this
   and under much pressure and tension
With the unfinished task of moving
   and problems too many to mention,
You finished it to surprise me,
   and there are no words to convey
The mixed and happy emotions
   my heart experienced today.

You're wonderful! You're marvelous! In fact, you are terrific. If I knew more swell adjectives, I'd be still more specific. Thank you, thank you, thank you.

Thanks to People Like You

There's something
   we should never forget—
That people we've known
   or heard of or met
By indirection have had
   a big part
In molding the thoughts
   of the mind and the heart—
And so it's people
   who are like you
That people like me
   should give thanks to,
For no one can win
   just on his own—
Too bad there aren't
   a whole lot more
People like YOU
   to be thankful for.

Thank you—what a lovely thing to do and just so very typical of you.

Many Thanks

Sometimes somebody does something so sweet
   it really sweeps you off your feet,
There are no words to express how you feel,
   for it's something too big for words to reveal!

You have an extra special way about you
   that makes everything you do extra special too!
That was the nicest thing to do—
   Many thanks to each one of you.

There are some that we meet in passing and forget as soon as they go. There are some we remember with pleasure and feel honored and privileged to know.

Memory Rendezvous

Memory builds a little pathway
    that goes winding through my heart,
It's a lovely, quiet, gentle trail
    from other things apart.
I only meet when traveling there
    the folks I like the best,
For this road I call remembrance
    is hidden from the rest.
But I hope I'll always find you
    in my memory rendezvous,
For I keep this little, secret place
    to meet with folks like you.

*Everyone needs someone, it certainly is true, and I'm very glad
and thankful to know someone like you.*

ℐ Love It!

Such greetings from a poet
   who's a master of expression,
Rise far above my just desserts
   and bring you this confession:
Your praise sets such a shining goal,
   I cannot reach or rise above it,
But lend an ear, and listen,
   "My goodness, how I love it!"

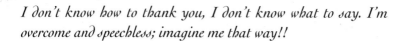

*I don't know how to thank you, I don't know what to say. I'm
overcome and speechless; imagine me that way!!*

A *Rare Gift*

To you who have been so kind to me
   I'm just as embarrassed as I can be
That I'm so tardy and so remiss
   in sending a great big thank-you kiss,
For that is exactly what I would do
   if I were in hugging distance of you,
For a Cadillac car or a sable coat,
   or a million dollar government note
Could not have pleased me as much as you did,
   for I was as tickled as a little kid,
When you brought me the orchid bouquet
   and shook your head when I started to pay
And said, "Mrs. Rice, these orchids are free,
   they're a little remembrance from my mom
     and me,"
And that is what made them seem even more rare
   to have them presented by such a sweet pair,
And each time I use one I'll think lovingly
   of the dear sweet ladies who gave them to me.

I may be late and running behind, but I've never had you off my mind. And I've been thankful every minute since I peeked in the box and saw what was in it.

Heartfelt Thanks

We can't pay God for sunshine,
    but in our meager way
We can offer Him our heartfelt thanks
    with each new dawning day.
And I can never pay you
    for your kind and lovely thought,
But I can thank you with my heart
    for the inner joy it brought.

I wish I could wrap appreciation, admiration, and affection all up into a nice gift package and send it to you as tangible evidence of my grateful heart and mixed emotions, for an expression of kindness always makes my heart sing.

More than you know,
I thank God up above
For fans, friends, and family,
and their gifts of love.

My heart rejoices,
and I'm thankful, too,
That I could share
this book with you.

For all of my poems
are woven of
Words that I borrow
from God up above.

HSR

What a blessing is the gift of expressing
Thanks from a thankful heart.
In doing so, we come to know
That appreciation is truly an art.

So, although this book has ended,
May thanks continue to flow,
For an attitude of gratitude
Encourages peace and love to grow.

vjr